This book has been produced to welcome you to the Holy Cross Monastery of Kilbroney, the first new Benedictine monastery in Northern Ireland for 800 years, built in the beautiful valley of Saint Bronagh's Church. With Christ at the heart of their daily lives and hospitality to all as their abiding principle, the community here offer a calming refuge of healing spirituality to those of all faiths and none.

For me personally it has become a very special place. Indeed I believe the Benedictine ethos and the deep sense of spirituality I encountered here was central to finding my way to faith. It was here that I took the first tentative steps on my journey, making my way to the monastery each Friday evening for two years to receive spiritual direction. From an agnostic background, still troubled by difficult questions and doubts, my path was made easier by the integrity, patience and insight with which those questions were answered. That, I would learn, is the way of the community here.

But, ultimately, what brought me over that unseen barrier to faith was simple if momentous. I was gently guided to the God of love, for what makes Holy Cross special is that God's Word is lived here, not merely spoken. Compassion, generosity and tolerance are not just preached but practised. Equally, intolerance, materialism and the abuse of power, from whatever quarter it comes, are robustly countered.

I was first sent to Holy Cross by a Protestant friend who knew the community well and would be a witness at my baptism here. It was fitting that the community first moved to the newly built monastery for the Week of Prayer for Christian Unity in 2004.

Reconciliation between Christians in Northern Ireland is central to the mission of the Rostrevor Benedictines. To find a place where Christians of different denominations can worship together is a greatly treasured gift in Northern Ireland, where decades of division and trauma have hardened hearts and undermined trust. You will find many testimonies from friends of the monastery in this book that underline the importance of this work.

Over the next pages, you will read how a small group of monks from the Abbey of Bec in Normandy, France began their mission to help bring unity to a divided land. In doing so they have created a place where we can all meet God as one and where His presence can be deeply felt. **Welcome to Holy Cross**.

Seth Linder
February 2011

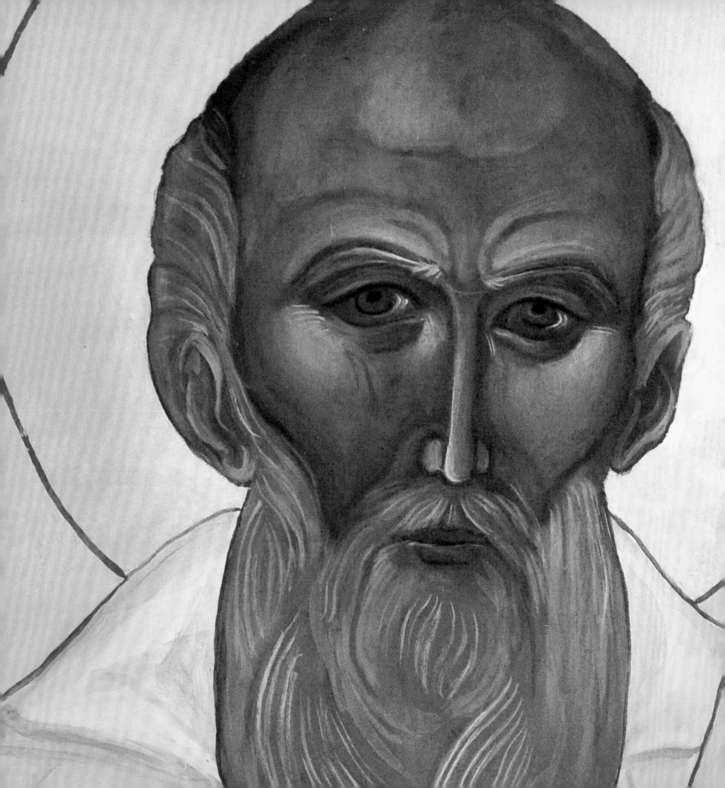

SAINT **BENEDICT**

Born in Umbria in 480 AD, Saint Benedict left his studies in Rome, disillusioned with what he saw as the city's degenerate lifestyle, to live as a hermit in the mountains of Subiaco. He later established twelve communities of monks there before founding a monastery at Monte Cassino in southern Italy. Here, instead of the normal small, separate communities of monks, he gathered his disciples into one large community, the first time this had happened. The Rule he wrote for the monks of Monte Cassino established the spirituality and way of life for all monastic communities to this day. Saint Benedict died in 547AD.

THE **BENEDICTINE** ORDER

Each independent house of the Benedictine Order is a separate family ruled by an Abbot and with its own noviciate (the provision of training for a prospective monk prior to taking vows). While each monastery will have its specific character, common characteristics will be found in all Benedictine houses whether of monks or nuns. Christ will be at the centre of all things and each community will strive to attain a balance between prayer (public liturgy, *lectio divina*, and personal prayer), work and study.

ST MARY OF **MONTE OLIVETO**

There are now twenty-one congregations within the Benedictine Confederation. The Rostrevor Benedictines belong to the Congregation of St Mary of Monte Oliveto, which was founded by Saint Bernard Tolomei, who established the Archabbey of Monte Oliveto Maggiore in the 13th century.

Since the time of their founder Olivetans have been clothed in white, following a vision in which Saint Bernard saw a vision of monks, each dressed in white, climbing a stairway to heaven, where Jesus and his Holy Mother awaited. A special characteristic of the Olivetan reform is its emphasis upon the spirit of communion uniting all its houses, called to form *unum corpus* - one body. The Congregation has a presence in Italy, France, the United Kingdom, Ireland, Belgium, Switzerland, Israel, Korea, USA, Mexico, Guatemala, Brazil and Ghana.

CHAPTER ONE

THE STORY OF THE **ROSTREVOR** BENEDICTINES

*they make the valley
a place of springs* PS 84:6

> **"What is the secret of the brothers in Rostrevor? Rooted in their life of prayer together, they offer an open, welcoming and healing place for so many different people, a place of communion. A sign of hope in our broken world! The Holy Cross as the Tree of Life. Isn't that the heart of all "prayer weavings" and struggles for peace and reconciliation? The Risen Christ, through the humble gift of their lives, goes on sowing his Easter seeds!"**

SISTERS OF GRANDCHAMP (PROTESTANT MONASTIC COMMUNITY IN SWITZERLAND)

go to the land that I will show you GENESIS 12:1

The monks of the foundation community of the most recent Benedictine Monastery in Ireland, at Rostrevor, Co Down, all made their monastic profession in the famous Abbey of Bec in Normandy.

Among the most illustrious sons of Bec, which was founded in 1034, are the great reformer of ecclesiastical life in England, Blessed Lanfranc, and the even better known philosopher-theologian, Saint Anselm. Both these men were to become Archbishops of Canterbury in their turn. At this time Bec was the most important school of Christendom in Europe. It ceased to be a monastery during the French Revolution but was restored to monastic life by Dom Paul M. Grammont, OSB (1911-1989) in 1948.

Building on the historic links between Bec and the See of Canterbury, as well as with so many other English bishoprics and abbeys, Dom Paul M. Grammont sought from that time onwards to foster and develop ecumenical relationships with the Church of England.

In recognition of the contribution the Abbey of Bec had made to the establishment and growth of ecumenical relations with the Anglican Communion, Dom Paul M. Grammont was invited by Archbishop Robert Runcie to participate in the historic meeting between John-Paul II and himself at Canterbury Cathedral on the eve of Pentecost, 1982.

OUR **FIRST MONASTIC PRESENCE** IN NORTHERN IRELAND

A chance encounter at Canterbury between the Abbot and the then Archbishop of Armagh, Cardinal Tomás Ó Fiaich, made a profound impact upon the former, awakening within him a spiritual intuition which would eventually lead to the establishment of a 'cella' of Bec in the Diocese of Down and Connor. This gesture of communion had been initiated following a retreat made with the Protestant monastic community of Grandchamp in Switzerland during the Week of Prayer for Christian Unity in January 1983. From August of that year until May 1987 monks from Le Bec-Hellouin lived a hidden life of prayer in the region of Downpatrick and the Ards. In this first outreach to Northern Ireland the monks were given the encouragement and help of the then Bishop of Down and Connor, Most Reverend Cahal Daly.

Jesus Christ is himself the cornerstone.

(Ephesians 2:20)

> *To undertake to pose this gesture of communion is about honouring our ecumenical vocation. This concrete gesture is to be understood as being in profound accord with and in the true spirit of our monastic calling. Our intention is to establish in Northern Ireland a discreet presence of prayer, where the monks will live in profound communion with the local Church, creating a place of reconciliation in this martyred land, interceding for the unity of the Church and the peace of this people, together with that of the whole world.*
>
> DOM PAUL M. GRAMMONT (ABBEY OF BEC-HELLOUIN, 31.03.1983)

Sadly, due to changing circumstances at Bec, the 'cella' in Northern Ireland had to be closed one year after Dom Paul M. Grammont retired. This closure was deeply regretted by the local Church and those Christians with whom the small Benedictine community had managed to enter into contact.

hope does not disappoint
ROMANS 5:5

Despite their bitter disappointment at the withdrawal of the monks, many people in Northern Ireland expressed their firm hope that one day, in God's own good time, a monastic presence of the Benedictine Order would be re-established in their midst. Writing in the Irish News at the time of Dom Paul M. Grammont's death in 1989, Bishop Cahal Daly spoke of the passing of this great figure of the French Church and 20th century monasticism as the loss of a distinguished abbot and friend to Ireland. Expressing his personal opinion and that of so many friends of the monks of Bec in Ireland, Bishop Daly spoke of their return to France as something deeply unfortunate, while going on to state his fervent hope that one day their presence would be resumed.

Speaking at the Eucharistic celebration to mark the twentieth anniversary of the date Bec monks were first sent to Ireland, on the Solemnity of the founder of the Olivetan Congregation, Blessed Bernard Tolomei, August 19th 2003, Cardinal Daly spoke of the fulfilment of Dom Paul M. Grammont's dream and the realisation of God's promise, summed up in the deceased abbot's abbatial motto: *Spes autem non confundit... Hope does not disappoint (Rm 5:5).*

the call of the Irish...come and walk among us once again CONFESSIONS OF SAINT PATRICK

The return of Olivetan Benedictine monks to Ireland came about as a result of a very specific call addressed to monasteries of contemplative life by John-Paul II:

> *In a special way, I entrust to monasteries of contemplative life the spiritual ecumenism of prayer, conversion of heart, and charity. To this end I encourage their presence wherever Christian communities of different confessions live side by side, so that their total devotion to the 'one thing needful' (cf. Lk 10:42) – to the worship of God and to intercession for the salvation of the world, together with their witness of evangelical life according to their special charisms – will inspire everyone to abide, after the image of the Trinity, in that unity which Jesus willed and asked of the Father for all his disciples.*

JOHN PAUL II (APOSTOLIC EXHORTATION VITA CONSECRATA, N.101)

A NEW **MONASTIC MISSION**

Dom Michelangelo M. Tiribilli, Abbot General of the Benedictine Congregation of Saint Mary of Monte Oliveto, recognised this call of the Church as corresponding with the earlier intuition which had led the Abbey of Bec to engage itself in Northern Ireland.

During the course of the canonical visitation to Bec-Hellouin in November 1997, the possibility of taking up the challenge of establishing a monastic presence in Northern Ireland was examined anew. A process of dialogue with those who felt willing to respond to the Pope's call led the Abbot General to designate the five monks who formed the foundation community of Rostrevor for this specific monastic mission. Their being sent to Ireland was to be the Olivetan Congregation's response to the invitation of *Vita Consecrata*.

"*The warmest and truest testimony I can give to the ministry of the Holy Cross Monastery in Rostrevor is that it is my 'second home'. I look forward to times of retreat there, both on a personal level and for my clergy and ordinands. But most of all, I meet the Lord Jesus there – in the hospitality of the monks, in the God-centredness of the worship and in the powerful ministry of the Word. It has been a joy and a blessing to be associated with the Benedictines since they arrived in Rostrevor and to be part of re-establishing a link, as their 'other bishop', with the Benedictine foundation which is Down Cathedral.*"

RT REV HAROLD MILLER (CHURCH OF IRELAND BISHOP OF DOWN AND DROMORE)

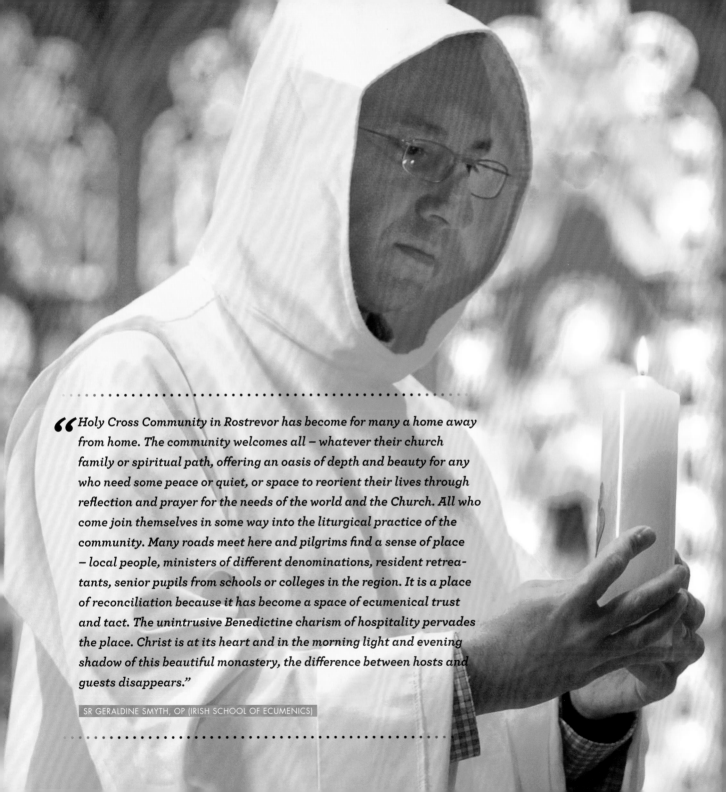

> *Holy Cross Community in Rostrevor has become for many a home away from home. The community welcomes all – whatever their church family or spiritual path, offering an oasis of depth and beauty for any who need some peace or quiet, or space to reorient their lives through reflection and prayer for the needs of the world and the Church. All who come join themselves in some way into the liturgical practice of the community. Many roads meet here and pilgrims find a sense of place – local people, ministers of different denominations, resident retreatants, senior pupils from schools or colleges in the region. It is a place of reconciliation because it has become a space of ecumenical trust and tact. The unintrusive Benedictine charism of hospitality pervades the place. Christ is at its heart and in the morning light and evening shadow of this beautiful monastery, the difference between hosts and guests disappears.*

SR GERALDINE SMYTH, OP (IRISH SCHOOL OF ECUMENICS)

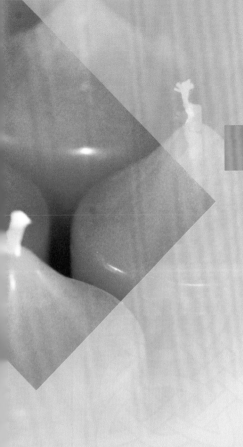

GO FORTH WITH **MY BLESSING**

Before leaving for Northern Ireland, the five monks were addressed by Dom Michelangelo at Monte Oliveto Maggiore, the Mother-House and cradle of the Olivetan monastic family.

> *At the end of your pilgrimage to the source of our Congregation, which is the Archicenobium of Monte Oliveto Maggiore, I feel the need to assure you of my paternal proximity as you set out upon your monastic experience in Northern Ireland. (...) To give a testimony of reconciliation in the martyred land of Ulster, as monks, is a mission of great importance in line with the intuition of the renowned Abbot Paul M. Grammont. Especially at the early stages difficulties will not be lacking. A constantly renewed spirit of sacrifice will be required of each one of you. With the most intense prayer I confide you to the intercession of Our Lady of Holy Hope, our Holy Father, Saint Benedict, and the Founder of our Congregation, Blessed Bernard Tolomei ... along with those great Irish saints, Patrick and Columbanus. You go forth with my blessing!*
>
> DOM MICHELANGELO M. TIRIBILLI, MONTE OLIVETO MAGGIORE, 30.12.1997

*may all
be one* JOHN 17:21

Ecumenical engagement is very much in accord with the Olivetan charism which particularly emphasises the promotion of a spirituality of communion. Each Olivetan community seeks to live in warm fraternal communion, bound to all the other communities of the Congregation in a strong family spirit of solidarity, forming *unum corpus, one body.*

Over a long period many Olivetan Monasteries throughout the world have shown a real commitment to participation in the Church's ecumenical endeavour. Indeed, some communities have been pioneers, showing commitment to ecumenical outreach long before the Second Vatican Council. Consideration of this important aspect of the Olivetan Congregation's monastic ministry led the General Chapter of 1998 to make a resolution whereby it engaged itself to further promote ecumenical endeavour in response to a frequently renewed call of the Magisterium to the Benedictine Order.

BRINGING **RECONCILIATION**

The Rostrevor Foundation, which is the fruit of a long and rich tradition of ecumenical engagement, was designated especially for this ecumenical mission. The Foundation Decree of Holy Cross Monastery states:

> *The aim of the Community of Holy Cross Monastery is to live the monastic life according to the charism of our Benedictine Congregation of Saint Mary of Monte Oliveto. Its particular mission is to contribute to reconciliation between Catholics and Protestants in a land marked by reciprocal violence and stained by the blood of Christian brothers and sisters.*

wherever they make you welcome...stay there LUKE 10:8

Mandated by the Definitory of the Olivetan Congregation, Dom Mark-Ephrem M. Nolan, OSB (first Superior) and Dom Eric M. Loisel, OSB, were sent across to Ireland to make an exploratory visit and consult with the Bishops of the North. They received a particularly warm welcome from the Bishop of Dromore, Most Reverend Francis Gerard Brooks (1924-2010).

With the Bishop's accord the five monks designated for the foundation arrived in Northern Ireland in January 1998 and took up residence in the former Retreat Centre of the Missionary Sisters of Our Lady of Apostles, Rostrevor. In September 1998 Dr Brooks issued, for the attention of the Olivetan General Chapter 1998, a letter of recognition of the new community temporarily established at the OLA Convent, Rostrevor, and expressed his hope that, as soon as a permanent location be found for the establishment of the community, the canonical erection of the monastery would take place.

INTRODUCTION TO IRISH LIFE

The monks had to learn patience, for it was some time before a permanent home could be found to house the community. Indeed, the decision was eventually taken to proceed to the canonical erection of the monastery even before the monks acquired their own property.

The waiting time spent in the former Retreat Centre of the OLA Sisters proved to be greatly beneficial to the monks – especially the French brethren who were introduced to the Irish way of life by this group of Missionary Sisters who had retired back to Ireland having spent lifetimes in Africa. These former missionaries were deeply conscious of the importance of helping the French monks adjust to life in what had become their adopted land.

they won the favour of all the people   ACTS 2:47

Within a very short space of time the monks' presence in Rostrevor came to people's attention. Not only local Catholics but Christian brothers and sisters from across the denominational divide soon started frequenting the daily liturgies celebrated by the community. Contacts were made with the local Protestant clergy and these have led to a remarkable fellowship which has seen former walls of separation fall. Since the beginning of 1999 ministers of all the local churches have been meeting with the Benedictine monks on a fortnightly basis for the shared prayer of the Sacred Scriptures in the monastic tradition of *lectio divina*. Out of this initiative, at clergy level, relationships have developed among all the People of God. The monastery has become a focal point and place of encounter for all the Churches of the area and from far beyond.

the people rejoiced, God having given them good cause for rejoicing
NEHEMIAH 12:43

Events in the life of the Benedictine community since the monks' arrival in Rostrevor have been regarded as celebrations for the wider Christian family and welcomed by all as an eloquent testimony to their commitment to live in communion with the local Church. The Solemn Profession of one brother and the ordination of another were particularly striking in this respect. Both these liturgies were celebrated in Kilbroney Parish Church, given the limited space in the OLA Convent Chapel. A large delegation from the other Christian Churches participated in these liturgies.

A 9th century bell from Saint Bronagh's Monastery, which is now enshrined in Saint Mary's Star of the Sea Church, was rung at the opening of both these celebrations, recalling the rich monastic heritage of the area in time past, while looking forward to its renewal through the Benedictine community's establishment in the Valley of Kilbroney. On the first occasion little did the congregation gathered suspect that hope had been given to the monks that they would in fact be staying in the Parish of Rostrevor, where they had already experienced such a warm welcome. Within a short space of time they were to learn this good news.

I will give you the land on which you lie
GENESIS 28:13

On October 23rd, 2000, the feast of Our Lady of Holy Hope, a patronal feast for the French branch of the Olivetan Congregation, a local farmer and his wife made an extremely generous offer of land to the monks for the building of a monastery. Around nine acres (about half of the farmer's small holding) were given to the community. Having discerned this gift to be a sign of the Lord's providential care and the indication of His will that a new monastery should be built in Kilbroney, the monks accepted this donation and set out in faith on a fund-raising campaign.

"To visit Holy Cross Monastery is to come to a place of welcome, prayer and peace set in a beautiful valley of God's wonderful creation. To stay at the monastery is to experience generous hospitality and gentle care gladly given. The daily pattern of worship through praise, prayer and the sacrament of Holy Communion while taking time to reflect on the meaning of God's love and word, is to know blessing and joy. To leave the monastery is to find that we have been strengthened for the journey of life ahead with a deeper commitment to follow in the steps of Christ Jesus, along the Pilgrim Way."

REV WINSTON GRAHAM (FORMER PRESIDENT OF THE METHODIST CHURCH, IRELAND)

"Holy Cross is a special place where we are embraced in warm friendship, refreshed by generous hospitality and refocused by the deep spirituality. The Word of God and the Spirit of God are living realities among these men of God. The highest compliment that we can pay is that we feel at home there."

REV DESI AND HEATHER MAXWELL (MINISTER OF THE PRESBYTERIAN CHURCH - XPLORATIONS)

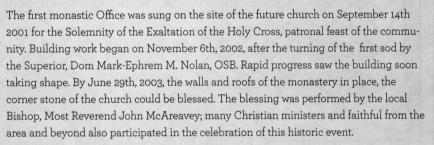

On March 21st, 2001, encouraged by their Abbot
General to *seek first the kingdom in the assurance that a
good providence would supply for their needs*, the Rostrevor
Benedictines launched their initial appeal for help. At the same
time they drew up architectural plans for the new monastery.

"let us build", and with willing hands they set about the good work   NEHEMIAH 2:18

The first monastic Office was sung on the site of the future church on September 14th
2001 for the Solemnity of the Exaltation of the Holy Cross, patronal feast of the community. Building work began on November 6th, 2002, after the turning of the first sod by
the Superior, Dom Mark-Ephrem M. Nolan, OSB. Rapid progress saw the building soon
taking shape. By June 29th, 2003, the walls and roofs of the monastery in place, the
corner stone of the church could be blessed. The blessing was performed by the local
Bishop, Most Reverend John McAreavey; many Christian ministers and faithful from the
area and beyond also participated in the celebration of this historic event.

The overall building project was completed just on time for the official opening of the
monastery and Solemn Consecration of the church for the first day of the Week of
Prayer for Christian Unity, January 18th, 2004.

hear the entreaty of your people as they pray in this place...hear and forgive   1 KINGS 8:29-30

The eve of the Solemn Dedication was marked by an Ecumenical Prayer Vigil.
The Service opened with the icon of the Holy Cross being carried into the new church
building by the Roman Catholic Bishop of Dromore (Most Reverend John McAreavey)
and the Church of Ireland Bishop of Down and Dromore (Right Reverend Harold Miller).

This symbolic gesture spoke of their commitment to bear witness to Christ together and demonstrated their mutual appreciation of the role the monastery seeks to play as a house of prayer for all peoples.

Lord Carey of Clifton, former Archbishop of Canterbury, preached the first sermon in the monastery church in which he concentrated on the vital role this place and the community it houses would have to play in furthering understanding and encouraging encounter between Christians of different traditions.

A **SAFE PLACE** FOR ALL

Rev. Canon Trevor Williams, former leader of the Corrymeela Community of Reconciliation (consecrated Anglican bishop of Limerick July 11th, 2008) spoke movingly of his experience of the community of Holy Cross as *a safe space where people from different backgrounds have already been led to come together and in their meeting share their stories with one another in an atmosphere of confidence and trust. This sharing has helped many not only to grow in mutual understanding and respect but also to experience healing of deep wounds from their troubled past.*

COMMITMENT TO **PEACE-MAKING**

Testimonies to the power of forgiveness through the experience of the cross were given by Rev. Bert Armstrong, a Methodist, whose brother and sister-in-law were killed by the IRA in the Enniskillen bomb (1987) and Michael McGoldrick, a Roman Catholic, whose only son was killed by the UVF in 1996 as part of the Drumcree stand-off. Many victims of over three decades of violence in Northern Ireland were present at this Prayer Vigil and found it to be a profoundly healing experience. An Act of Repentance and a joint commitment to peace-making was led by the Superior of the Monastery and the local Church of Ireland and Presbyterian Ministers.

My house shall be a house of prayer for all

ISAIAH 56:7

The Solemn Dedication, the following day, brought together many distinguished representatives of the Church in Ireland and the Church Universal of both the Roman Catholic and Protestant traditions. Representatives of the monastic communities of both the Benedictine and Cistercian Orders, together with representatives of other forms of Consecrated Life, including Sisters from the Protestant Monastic Community of Grand-champ in Switzerland, also came to express their solidarity with the nascent monastery.

This Eucharistic celebration opened with the presentation of the original stone water font from Down Cathedral by the Dean of the Chapter, V. Rev. John Dinnen, as a sign of love and prayerful communion in one Lord, one faith, one baptism. The Roman Catholic and Church of Ireland Bishops united to sprinkle the people, walls and altar of the church with the blessed water. The ambo of the new church was consecrated by Archbishop George Carey, followed by the proclamation of the Scripture readings by ministers of the Presbyterian and Methodist traditions.

A JOURNEY **TO UNITY**

In his homily Bishop John McAreavey expressed his hopes and expectations for the community in these terms:

> *The Benedictines value in a special way stability, stability in the long tradition behind them and stability in the place where their monastery is situated. It seems to me that this stability gives them freedom to set out on journeys that involve risk and that break new ground. And so the wider Church looks to this community to become a community of reconciliation and, in a way, to blaze a trail that the rest of us might follow. We look to you to help us to journey from an attitude of separateness to one of partnership; we look to you to help us make the journey from detachment from the fate of other Christians to a sense of deep care about what is happening to them. There is a journey that we have to make from privacy to trust that allows us to share our own personal and Church concerns with our brothers and sisters in other Church communities. Above all, we have to journey from a tolerance of division to a deep sense of the scandal of Christian divisions. We look to you to make us uncomfortable in many of the attitudes we take and to show us the way to a better future.*

After the anointing of the altar table, the consecration stones of the church were anointed by the local Bishop, the Apostolic Nuncio – Dr Guiseppe Lazzaroto, the Roman Catholic Primate of All Ireland – Archbishop Sean Brady, Bishop Francis Gerard Brooks, the Olivetan Abbot General – Archabbot Michelangelo M. Tiribilli, OSB, and the monastery's Founding Father, Dom Mark-Ephrem M. Nolan, OSB. It was Cardinal Cahal Daly who inaugurated the Blessed Sacrament Chapel, placing the Reserved Sacrament in the tabernacle at the end of this first Eucharist to be celebrated in the church.

"The monastic community in Rostrevor offers a genuine welcome and hospitality to all. Silence permeates and draws one deeper into self where God awaits with infinite longing. The meditative recital of the psalms with the community and the choice of readings and commentaries clarify and enlarge God's communication with one. The Eucharist is clearly the highlight of the day when one becomes the Body of Christ and hears his words applied with unction to life. Meals are a true extension of the Eucharist, maintaining the contemplative attention to the guest, the food and the reading."

SR CONCHITA MCDONNELL, MSHR (CORI - CONFERENCE OF RELIGIOUS IN IRELAND)

"It is a great blessing for us in the North of Ireland to have your monastery in our midst as a centre of renewal in the Spirit. One finds in the monastery an atmosphere of prayer and of true community which is difficult to find anywhere else in today's world. The setting of the monastery, its lovely, peaceful and verdant valley, is so conducive to the monastic presence.

It would be difficult to find anywhere a setting better adapted for monastic life; I have often spoken of Kilbroney as 'a valley waiting for its monastery'. It seems to me to be just the kind of location which was sought out by monks down the ages – such as Clonmacnois or Glendalough in Ireland, or Citeaux in France. May it continue to be blessed by God and to be a blessing for God's people as these famous ancient monasteries were."

H. E. CARDINAL CAHAL B. DALY (1917-2009)

they are happy who dwell in your house PS 84:4

The community has been happily settled into its permanent home since January 2004. An ever-increasing number of visitors to Holy Cross Monastery are delighted to discover this fine complex of buildings nestled in the picturesque foothills of the Mournes. The monastery fits into the landscape as if it has always been there. The exterior and interior design are, at one and the same time, stark in their simplicity and noble in their beauty. The building is filled with light throughout and the strategic placing of the windows has, as it were, established a kind of ongoing dialogue with the natural surroundings of the valley. Everything about the design speaks of harmony. This is particularly true of the interior of the church building – a fitting place of worship for a community whose mission is to live a parable of communion.

here God alone will be my intention… His love the subject of my contemplation ST ANSELM

More important than the buildings which house a community is the life it seeks to lead. Having been engendered by the French Benedictine tradition, the monks of Rostrevor lead a monastic life without any outside pastoral ministry. The sung liturgy is central to the monks' daily horarium – Gregorian chant and contemporary music in the vernacular (largely in-house composition) are used. A strong emphasis is placed upon *lectio divina* and personal prayer. Periods of silent prayer after the morning and evening Offices are shared in common. Manual work and study are also important features of the monks' daily routine.

The community supports itself by the making of handmade decorative candles and the production of greeting cards. All domestic duties are undertaken by the monks themselves. Hospitality is a significant aspect of Benedictine life and this is also true

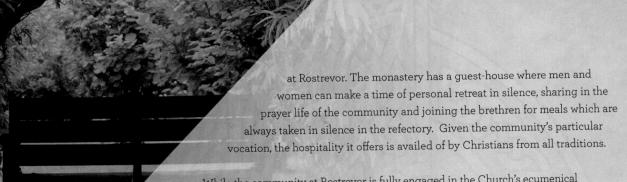

at Rostrevor. The monastery has a guest-house where men and women can make a time of personal retreat in silence, sharing in the prayer life of the community and joining the brethren for meals which are always taken in silence in the refectory. Given the community's particular vocation, the hospitality it offers is availed of by Christians from all traditions.

While the community at Rostrevor is fully engaged in the Church's ecumenical endeavour, its approach is less that of doing ecumenism than seeking to be by its whole way of life a living parable of reconciliation and a call to restored unity in Christ.

In March 2001, Dr McAreavey summed up his impressions of the contribution the Benedictines of Rostrevor have to make in the Irish Church in these lines written to endorse the monks' appeal for support:

> *At this point in the history of the Irish Church, I believe that this monastic presence is a gift of God to us. It enriches us with its tradition of contemplation nourished by the Scriptures, prayerful liturgy, a commitment to ecumenism and the task of reconciliation. I am confident that this community, which has put down roots in the Diocese of Dromore, will flourish and bear fruit abundantly.*

remember the rock from which you were hewn

ISAIAH 51:1

The late Dom Paul M. Grammont always emphasised the importance of remembering the first steps made in any project so as to remain faithful to its original intuition. The story of the post-Reformation restoration of Benedictine life to the North of Ireland began at Ballykilbeg in the Parish of Downpatrick, 800 years after Benedictine monks came to Down Cathedral from Chester, a Bec foundation.

In a letter addressed to Dom Paul M. Grammont in November 1983 to express his joy that monks from Bec had come to Northern Ireland, the Cardinal Tomás Ó Fiaich explained:

> *Ballykilbeg, where your monks have arrived, is associated with notable figures of Irish history. It was the birthplace of Archbishop William Crolly, the first Archbishop of Armagh after the penal times to reside in the city of Armagh and the prelate who began the building of Armagh Cathedral. It was also the place of residence of a famous Orange leader of the 19th century called Johnston and is therefore a name which is rich in memories for the Protestant people of Ulster. Please God it will be possible for your community to link together the two traditions, i.e. that of Crolly and that of Johnston, into one single Irish Christian tradition.*

He makes the two one

EPHESIANS 2:15

The community has been graced to be able to contribute in some small way to the linking together of the two traditions in this land. About half of those who come on retreat to the monastery come from the Protestant Churches, with the vast majority of the younger generation who frequent Holy Cross being drawn from a Protestant background. For many of these young people contact with the community has grown out of what has been referred to as the re-*monk*-ing of the Church or its rein-*habit*-ing. They are attracted by monasticism's radical response to the gospel; they are anxious to learn from the monks' centuries' long tradition of contemplative prayer and community living.

The monastery has become for people of all generations a centre in which the treasures of God's Word are opened up and explored through the daily proclamation of the Sacred Scriptures' message and teaching sessions. Many groups come on pilgrimage, while many individual Protestants or Protestant groups enter into their first contact with people of a Catholic background through frequentation of the monastery. All of this rejoices the monastic community greatly and confirms to us the need for places of encounter such as that provided here at Holy Cross.

you shall be my witnesses
ACTS 1: 8

While the monks' ecumenical ministry is lived by and large in the monastery itself, it should be noted that they are sometimes called upon to reach out beyond the confines of the monastery to bear witness to the values the monastic community seeks to live at Holy Cross day after day. Discernment is exercised in response to the calls addressed to the monastic community in order to avoid a dispersion which could detract from the monks giving authentic witness as a community of contemplative life. Clearly, the monks seek to honour the call of the Catholic Church *for consecrated persons to give more space in their lives to ecumenical prayer and genuine evangelical witness so that by the power of the Holy Spirit the walls of division and prejudice can be broken down.* (cf. Vita Consecrata 100.)

The Benedictine community of Rostrevor resonates with the declaration made by The Congregation for Institutes of Consecrated Life and Societies of Apostolic Life when it declares in its Instruction on Consecrated Life in the Third Millennium: *Starting afresh from Christ,* that *the sharing of 'lectio divina' and taking part in common prayer in which the Lord guarantees His presence are ways particularly suitable for members of monastic communities.*

There is no doubt that the gift of friendship which has been hailed and celebrated in the writings and by the example of so many monastic teachers over the centuries is one of the privileged ways by which God permits us to bear witness to His love and to manifest the truth that the monks of Holy Cross are continually given to experience: namely how *it is good and pleasant for brothers and sisters to be gathered together as one and to dwell in unity.* (cf. Ps 133[132])

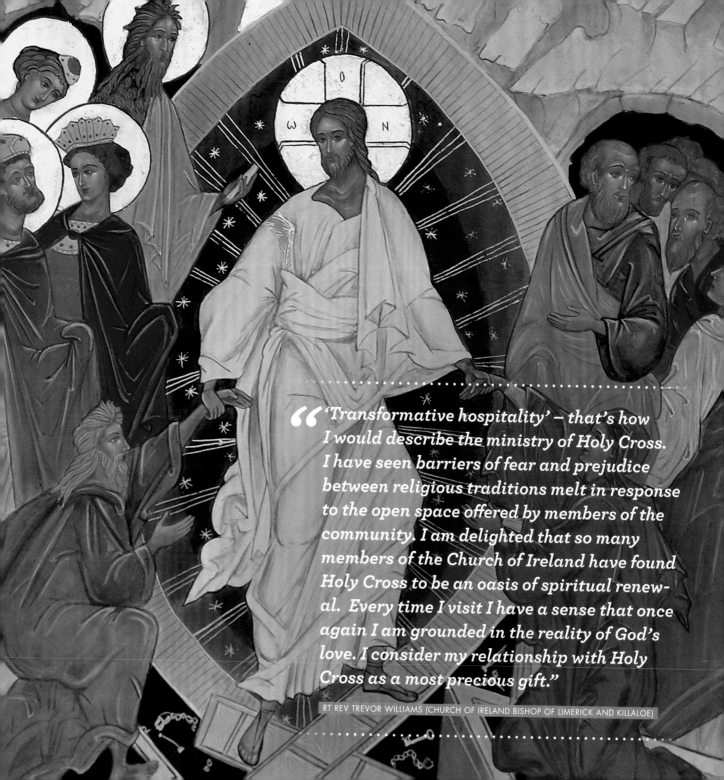

"'Transformative hospitality' – that's how I would describe the ministry of Holy Cross. I have seen barriers of fear and prejudice between religious traditions melt in response to the open space offered by members of the community. I am delighted that so many members of the Church of Ireland have found Holy Cross to be an oasis of spiritual renewal. Every time I visit I have a sense that once again I am grounded in the reality of God's love. I consider my relationship with Holy Cross as a most precious gift."

RT REV TREVOR WILLIAMS (CHURCH OF IRELAND BISHOP OF LIMERICK AND KILLALOE)

"To have a monastery in-sight and on-site of any place is a blessing. To have a Benedictine Monastery of the Olivetan Benedictine tradition is a gift. For Northern Ireland in these post war and trauma years to have the presence of monks chanting and praying ceaselessly in their midst is a real incarnation of peace. But most astounding is that this Holy Cross Monastery is dedicated to dialogue and the unity of all Christians. This work is not optional."

SR MEG FUNK, OSB (BEECH GROVE BENEDICTINES, INDIANA, USA)

On certain occasions and in some places, the monks' presence alone has made quite a strong statement in regard to the ecumenical journey being undertaken in Ireland. That a Roman Catholic Benedictine Monk should be the preacher at the Episcopal consecration of an Anglican Bishop (Dom Mark-Ephrem M. Nolan preached for the Consecration of Trevor Williams as Bishop of Limerick on Saint Benedict's day, July 11th, 2008) drew the attention of the national news. That a group of monks should be asked to participate in a festival gathering a few thousand young Evangelical Christians for teaching and worship (*Summer Madness 2010*) once again drew the attention of the Irish television network RTE. A whole host of similar events could be cited.

ring out our joy to the Lord   PS 81:1

For all these developments we feel that we can well and truly ring out our joy. An ecumenical gathering of clergy and faithful for the blessing of a set of three new bells for the bell tower of the monastery on the Solemnity of Saint Bernard Tolomei in August 2010 had us ring out our joy and celebrate together the theological virtues of faith, hope and love. It is these fundamental graces which hold the monks of Rostrevor, united with all God's People, committed to the journey to continue the path to unity together.

The new bells installed in the bell tower beside the church are dedicated to the memory of three witnesses who have been guiding lights upon the Rostrevor community's path because of their love for the Church and their desire to see all God's people gathered together in the spirit of communion. On the bell dedicated to the memory of Dom Paul M. Grammont, OSB, are inscribed these words, *Faith is the assurance of things hoped for... He saw and greeted the promise from afar* (Hebrews 11: 1.13), while on the bell in honour of Saint Mary, the Mother of Holy Hope, one reads *Hope does not disappoint us* (Romans 5:5),

finally the inscription on the bell ascribed to Saint Bernard Tolomei, to mark his recent canonisation, the message is a clear call for the community to participate in the mystery of its holy founder's self-giving love, *There is no greater love than to give one's life* (John 15:13).

The presence of brethren from our own monastic family, along with Archbishop Robert Le Gall, OSB, from the Diocese of Toulouse in France, who presided over the blessing of the bells, made this celebration a richly blessed and truly joyous occasion for the Rostrevor community. It bore testimony to the fact that we are called to live our ministry here in Rostrevor as part of the Church Universal, reaching out to and receiving from the whole Body of Christ and the great family of nations.

all peoples bless our God
PS 68:32

The international make-up of the community at Holy Cross is another important aspect of the Rostrevor community's testimony in an increasingly globalised world. It is surely significant that the community's first local recruit to make Profession for our monastery came all the way from Mexico, inspired greatly by the community's ecumenical monastic vision.

when I am lifted up from the earth I will draw all to myself
JOHN 12:32

In this world the cross of Jesus stands as the great rallying point, the source of our reconciliation and peace.

The fervent prayer of the monks of Rostrevor, who gather for worship several times a day below the icon of the cross which adorns their monastic church is summed up in the inscription written over the head of Christ on this icon: *May all be one.*

The cross is also held before our eyes as a reminder of our Christian calling to share in the compassion of Christ for the world. As they gather for prayer at several points throughout each day, the monks of Rostrevor seek to give echo to the cry of the world, presenting in their thanksgivings and intercessions the joys and sorrows, the hopes and tribulations of the whole world.

He by whom the good work was started will bring it to completion

PHILIPPIANS 1:6

We have shared something of our story with you in this short account of the origins of our community and the beginning of its life here in the Monastery of the Holy Cross in Kilbroney Valley. We are well aware that so much of our story is still unwritten because it has yet to be lived.

The following lines from the writings of the late Pope John-Paul II, which we share with you by way of conclusion at this juncture in the unfolding of our story, encourage us to look to the future with hope:

You have not only a glorious history to remember and to recount, but also a great history yet to be accomplished! Look to the future, where the Spirit is sending you in order to do even greater things (...). Be always faithful to Christ, the Church, to your Institute (monastery) and to the men and women of our time.

CHAPTER **TWO**

A **DAY IN THE LIFE** OF THE COMMUNITY

*From the rising of the
sun to its setting, praised
be the name of the Lord* PS 113:3

In the morning I offer you my prayer. (PS 5:3)

6.45AM

Speak, Lord, for your servant is listening. (1SAM 3:9)

8.30AM

To the Lord I will sing, I will make melody to the Lord. (JUDG 5:3)

9.30AM

By the labour of your hands you shall eat. (PS 128:2)

11.00AM

*They remained faithful to the brotherhood,
to the breaking of bread and to the prayers.* (AC 2:42)

11.30AM

11.30AM

Whether we eat or drink, let us proclaim Christ, pray to Christ, think of Christ, speak of Christ. (ST AMBROSE)

12.45AM

Monastic community...a grace of communion...coloured and tempered by the communal charism of brotherhood in pilgrimage and in hope. (THOMAS MERTON)

1.45PM

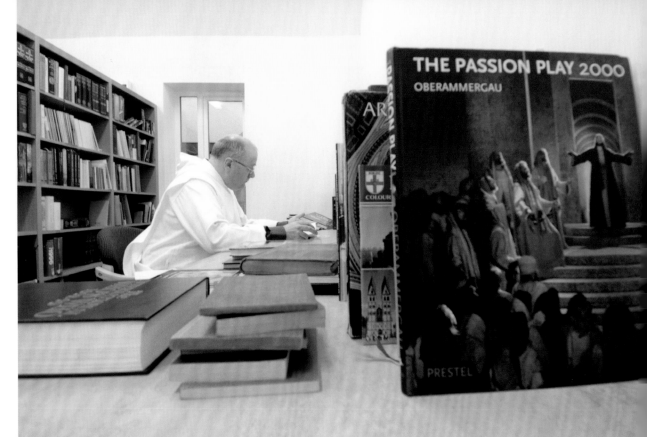

The brothers should have specified periods for manual labour as well as for prayerful reading. (RB 48:1)

2.30PM

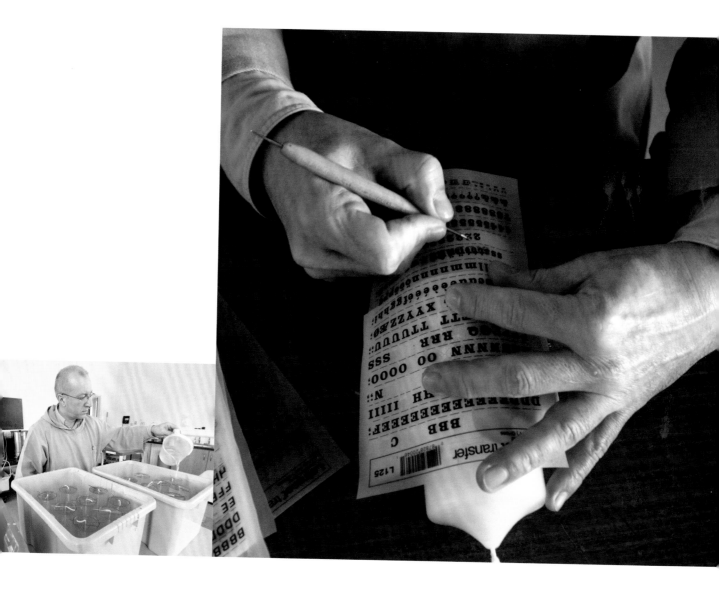

4.45PM

 5.30PM

The disciples said: "The day is almost over...the Lord went in, stayed with them and he was with them at the table. (LK 24:29-30)

6.45PM

8.30PM

Bless the Lord through the night. [PS 134:2]

9.15PM

CHAPTER **THREE**

THE
CHURCH

*Lord, listen to the prayer
that your servant will
offer in this place* 2CHR 6:20

The church building is the heart of the Monastery of the Holy Cross. Here the community, the resident guests and visitors meet with the Lord in prayer and are united with each other in the spirit of communion.

ONE LORD, ONE FAITH, ONE BAPTISM

ONE LORD ONE FAITH ONE BAPTISM

The first thing to greet the visitor in the porch of this modern church is an ancient stone holy water font. This stone, which comes from Down Cathedral, was a gift from the Church of Ireland Diocese of Down and Dromore as a sign of the fellowship we share. It was the original holy water font of Downpatrick Cathedral which would have already been in place when monks arrived there from Chester in England in 1183 to establish a Benedictine foundation at the behest of John de Courcy. Those 12th century monks came from a monastery which had been founded by the French Abbey of Bec under its abbot Saint Anselm. Therefore, there was already a connection between the Benedictine presence in Co Down and the Abbaye Notre-Dame du Bec-Hellouin, from whence the foundation community at Rostrevor came to Ireland in 1998. Above the stone holy water font one reads this message from Paul's Letter to the Ephesians: *One Lord, One Faith, One Baptism*. This inscribed plaque which immediately catches one's eye was a gift of the Church of Ireland Parish of Kilbroney.

Leaving the porch and entering the church proper one goes on to discover an interior design and furnishings which are striking in their simplicity and all deeply significant. The architecture itself and the discreet art work express the essence of the monastic community's vocation; they give visual form to its particular witness within the Church and before the world.

GATHERING, UNITY, **HARMONY**

The basic mandate given by the monks to their architect (Mr Brian Quinn of Rooney & McConville, Belfast) was that the church should reflect the concepts of gathering, unity, harmony and that all this should be expressed in a noble simplicity.

Soon a metaphor for the church building imposed itself on the architect. As he walked the green field site looking for inspiration he found himself continually attracted by a landmark which can be seen on a hillside just opposite the monastery: a circle of trees, planted around a mound of stones. Clearly, a fairy fort or ring fort, the spiritual significance attached to such places will be evident to anyone familiar with Irish traditions.

The architect's idea was to create a Christian sacred space inspired by this site of pre-Christian spiritual significance. One thinks of how Saint Benedict claimed for Christ the site to build his monastery at Monte Casino by erecting the monastic community's church where a pagan shrine had once stood.

The architect's original idea was to propose a circular building to correspond to the circle of trees, but there were disadvantages to this design. It was felt that in practical usage it would militate against the very thing it was meant to signify: gathering. Compromise was arrived at when the community suggested that an apse shaped choir area be adopted in the plan. This gives the visual impression of the circle to those who are in the nave of the church. They feel caught into the circular movement created by the monks gathered in the wide semi-circular apse in their curved choir stalls.

CROSS OF **LIGHT**

The wooden pillars holding up the roof of the church evoke the tree trunks of the wooded fairy fort, while the wooden panelling on the ceiling, decorated with openings through which light shines, evokes the sunlight which pours through the leaves of the trees.

The centre piece of the roof is a cruciform high window, creating a cross of light which is reflected in the communion cup when it is placed upon the altar for the celebration of Eucharist.

The main feature of the church is the simple, unadorned altar which symbolises the presence of Christ in the midst of His people. It is Christ who gathers together as one the monastic community and the people of God who join them for worship.

This altar is in Jerusalem stone, as are the twelve consecration stones which are on the walls around the church building. The use of Jerusalem stone (literally a large block of stone hewn from a rock in the Holy Land) reminds us of the Jewish roots of our Christian faith and speaks of our hope of rebirth for the Church by recalling the initial Pentecost event which brought the Church into being at Jerusalem.

THE **LIVING PASSION**

The most striking feature of the church for many is the large icon of the cross in Russian iconographic style which hangs above the ambo. The icon could be said to resume the vocation of the monastic community placed under the patronage of the Holy Cross. A closer examination of the icon reveals that while Christ is depicted nailed to the cross, His side has not yet been pierced by the lance. He is shown in this way to still be living His passion. The inscription above Christ's head upon this cross is a verse from John 17: *May all be one*. The icon is clearly born from a meditation on Jesus' Prayer for Unity. It is an invitation to the monastic community and all who look to it to enter into Christ's own intercession for the unity of His Church and to make of their lives a living offering for that same intention.

Just below the icon of the cross is the lectern from which the Word of God is proclaimed each time the monks gather in the church for prayer. Its central place signifies the centrality of the Sacred Scriptures in the monastic community's spirituality. The ambo was consecrated by Lord George Carey of Clifton, former Archbishop of Canterbury, while the altar was consecrated by Bishop John McAreavey of Dromore.

The unity theme is taken up in the tapestry which hangs behind the tabernacle containing the reserved sacrament. It is a hand-woven patchwork largely made by two people with special needs. They were asked to create the biggest panels of tapestry they could in different shapes and sizes, in different colours, using different fabrics and textures, but all blending together in harmony. The idea is that once sewn together they would represent the Church in her wide diversity, all pointing to and held together by Christ at the centre. The reserved sacrament was put in place for the first time on the day of the Dedication of the church by Cardinal Cahal B. Daly, a close friend of the Rostrevor community.

SEEING **GOD**

The windows of the church and *Salve cloister* are of modern design and were created by the architect in consultation with the community. They are composed of leaded glass, with some bevelled glass and some frosted glass panels. They define the space of the church building without confining it. In the church itself, as throughout the complex of monastic buildings, one is struck by the constant dialogue between inside and outside. From within the buildings one is constantly invited to see God and thank Him for the beauty of the natural surroundings in which the monastery is nestled.

KEEPING THE WORD **IN OUR HEARTS**

In the *Salve cloister* one finds an icon of the *Theotokos* before which the monks halt each evening at the end of the last prayer of the day before entering into the great silence of the night during which, like Mary, they keep silence so as to ponder the Word in their hearts.

CHAPTER **FOUR**

VOCATION

Here I am, Lord,
since you called me 1SAM 3:5

IS THE LORD CALLING YOU
TO **BECOME A MONK?**

Perhaps having read the story of the Rostrevor Benedictines and having been afforded a little glimpse into daily life at the monastery some readers might find themselves asking the question: *Could I be called to share in the life of this Benedictine community?*

If you are asking yourself this question then we would say to you: ***Consider your call*** (1Cor 1:26), ***taking the Gospel for your guide*** (Rule of Benedict, Prologue 21).

The Search for God

Saint Benedict asks of the one who presents himself at the door of the monastery: ***Does he truly seek God?*** (RB 58:8). Of course, before any of us ever set ourselves to seek God, He is searching for us: ***Seeking his workman in a multitude of people, the Lord calls out to him: Is there anyone here who yearns for life and desires to see good days? If you hear this and your answer is 'I do'*** (RB Prologue 14-16), then maybe the Lord is calling you to monastic life and you should explore things further.

The monk's search for God is fashioned by the gospel and is lived in response to the Lord's call to live in communion with Him and with others in the bond of mutual love.

BENEDICTINE **LIFE**

A Benedictine life evidently takes on the particular shape and form given to it by the Rule.

The *opus Dei* (the Divine Office), *lectio divina* (prayerful reading of the Scriptures), solitary prayer, reading, study and work are all essential elements of the search for God in monastic life. Sustained by all these practices the monk strives to live every moment of his life in an awareness of God's presence. We could say then that a monk is someone who, in response to God's call, strives to live constantly present to the one who is Presence.

A LIFE **IN COMMUNION**

While the monk is a man of communion, he draws strength for his life in communion with others through a serious and regular engagement in solitary prayer. Just as he strives to live present to the Presence, so he will seek out moments to be alone with the Alone.

CONVERSION, STABILITY AND OBEDIENCE

Essential to the Benedictine monastic vocation is the call to engage oneself with others. The Benedictine monk seeks God through community life under the guidance of a Superior. He commits himself to seek God in a life of ongoing conversion lived in stability and obedience.

THE LORD SPEAKS TO THOSE WHO LISTEN

Listening is absolutely fundamental to the whole process of monastic living. The opening word of the Rule sets the tone for everything that follows: *Listen!* (RB Prologue 1).

If we are to hear God's voice we have to learn to wait in silence and in humility of heart: *The disciple is to be silent and listen* (RB 6:6).

The monk will seek to *walk humbly* with God and with his brethren. Benedict sees humility as central to the monk's whole attitude in life (cf. Micah 6:8 & RB 7).

PREFER NOTHING TO **CHRIST**

Of course, everything in the Benedictine's life depends upon the monk fostering one fundamental relationship: his relationship with Christ to whom *nothing whatsoever is to be preferred* (RB 72).

Presence to Christ is inseparable from presence to all those who believe in Him, because we cannot separate Christ from the members of His body, the Church. For this reason the prayer of Jesus prayed on the eve of His passion for the unity of all His children is echoed by the monks of Rostrevor. At Holy Cross Monastery the community is firmly committed to pray with Christ: *May all may be one* (John 17). The desire for unity, peace and reconciliation is at the heart of their prayer, listening, community life, work and hospitality. The monastic community living in the bonds of mutual love by its united witness strives to be a leaven of unity in the dough of the divided Churches, *a parable of communion, a sign of humanity reconciled.*

THERE IS NO GREATER LOVE THAN TO **GIVE ONE'S LIFE**

The only way to understand monastic life is to see it for what it is essentially: participation in that unbounded generosity of Christ which led Him to give His life out of love.

The community of Rostrevor believes that a treasure has been confided to it which it is impelled to share with others. It is for this reason that it dares to promote its life with respect, with prayer and with the explicit invitation to others to accept the Lord's call to engage themselves within it.

To any reader who feels that the Lord may be calling him we would say: *if you hear God's call, do not reject it!* (John-Paul II VC 106).

And to those who are afraid of the cost involved in leaving all to follow Christ we would say: *whoever follows after Christ, the perfect man, becomes himself more of a man.* (Gaudium et Spes 41).

JOYFUL **WITNESS**

The world and the Church today long and call out for joyful witnesses to Christ. They need concrete signs of hope, disciples who are willing to follow the example of Christ who gave His life for others out of love.

MONKS OF **UNITY**

It is the desire and fervent prayer of the monastic community at Rostrevor that by the life we lead we may sow seeds of peace and fraternity in a troubled and fractured world and in a wounded and divided Church which needs to experience the healing grace of reconciliation.

A COMMUNITY OF **HOPE**

As monks who were confided the mission to bring the grace of holy hope to Ireland we believe that *Christ the hope of glory is in our midst (Col 1:27).*

Over long centuries in the ancient monastic valley of Kilbroney, from the time when the ancient well of Bronagh was opened to the fresh springs of living water which now flow at Holy Cross, God has shown Himself faithful to His people. We believe that He who has called us will remain faithful to His promise *to make us take root, be happy and prosper in the land to which He has guided us (Dt 5:33).*

And so we dare to hope that others will be led and strengthened by God's grace to give answer to the Risen Christ's final question and ultimate call: *Do you love me?... Follow me!* We call upon those who hear this call to join us on our pilgrim way.

> *"Do not be afraid! Open wide the doors for Christ! If we let Christ into our lives, we lose nothing, nothing, absolutely nothing of what makes life free, beautiful and great. No! Only in this friendship are the doors of life opened wide. Only in this friendship is the great potential of human existence truly revealed... Dear young people: do not be afraid of Christ! He takes nothing away and he gives you everything. When we give ourselves to him, we receive a hundred-fold in return. Yes, open, open wide the doors to Christ - and you will find true life."*

BENEDICT XVI (VERBUM DOMINI, N. 104)

CHAPTER FIVE

HOSPITALITY

Welcome one another as Christ welcomed you RM 15:7

COME AWAY FOR A WHILE

The Benedictine Monks of Holy Cross Monastery are happy to welcome guests in their midst for a time of retreat and spiritual renewal.

While it is often remarked that people increasingly feel the need to escape the pressures of life in today's busy and frenetic world it is interesting to note that as early as the 11th century Saint Anselm, writing at the Abbey of Bec, could pen these words:

> *Come on now, little one, get away from your worldly occupations for a while, escape from your tumultuous thoughts. Lay aside your burdensome cares and put off your laborious exertions. Give yourself over to God for a little while, and rest for a while in Him. Enter into the cell of your mind, shut out everything except God and whatever helps you to seek Him once the door is shut. Speak now, my heart, and say to God, "I seek your face; your face, Lord, I seek".*

ST ANSELM, PROSLOGION CH. 1

> *When God's voice is drowned out by incessant clamour, whether inner or outer, in whatever shape or form, then continuous dialogue with God becomes impossible. An inner monologue with myself, constant chatter with others, the invasion of the spoken word through the press and television are all the ever-present realities in my daily life over which I need to exercise some sort of discipline if I am to keep any quiet inner space in which to listen to the Word.*

ESTHER DE WAAL, A LIFE-GIVING WAY

LISTEN IN THE SILENCE

To help their guests to meet with God the monks of Holy Cross Monastery offer a space of silence which all who come to share in their life for some days are invited to respect. Silence is maintained in the guest-house, while the midday and evening meals are taken in silence with the monastic community in the refectory.

SHARE WITH **A BROTHER**

During their stay at the monastery guests may meet with a brother to share with him what they are experiencing during their time of retreat. Others may seek counsel or sacramental reconciliation. The community welcomes these requests and sees this spiritual accompaniment as part of its ministry.

UNITE IN **PRAYER**

Guests are invited to share in the prayer life of the community. We have seen how the monks gather in the church several times a day for the celebration of the liturgy; it is suggested that guests attend some of these times of worship.

REFRESHED, **GO IN PEACE**

The community hopes that all who come to the monastic guest-house benefit from the time they spend at the monastery and it rejoices greatly when they learn that a time of retreat has proved beneficial for a guest.

"A brother came to visit a monk.
As he was taking his leave, he said:
'Pardon me, father, for I have caused you to violate your rule.'
But the monk answered:
'My rule is to refresh you and send you back in peace."

Finally, pray for us 2 THESS. 3:1

I take this opportunity to invite you who have entered into contact with the Rostrevor community through this publication to hold its life and ministry in your prayer.

Pray that we may remain faithful to our calling; intercede with and for us that we may grow in depth and number, so as to be able to serve God in this place for a long time to come.

**Dom Mark-Ephrem M. Nolan, OSB,
Benedictine Monks, Holy Cross Monastery.**